HOW TO STAY OUT OF JAIL

TURNING FROM YOUR WAY TO GOD'S WAY

Written by
PATRICK DAY

Illustrated by Myron Sahlberg

PYRAMID
Publishers

Copyright © 2018
Patrick Day and Myron Sahlberg

Minneapolis, Minnesota
www.pyramidpublishers.com

All rights reserved. No part of this publication
may be reproduced, stored in a retrieval system,
or transmitted, in any form or by any means,
electronic, mechanical, photocopying,
recording, or otherwise, without the prior
written permission of the author.

Printed by
Lightning Source 1246 Heil Quaker Blvd.
La Vergne, TN USA 37086

ISBN – 978-0-9982014-1-2

Cover, Page Design and Illustrations
by Myron Sahlberg

Printed in the United States of America

All Scripture verses are taken from
The Message unless otherwise noted.

CHAPTER ONE
I Turned from My Way to God's Way

MY NAME IS PATRICK DAY. I'M A GIDEON who visits jails and rehab centers mainly in Minnesota. But this is not my story. It's your story.

You've been in and out of jails more than once, perhaps more times than you care to remember. You want to turn your life around, but you can't help yourself. You want to do good, but you commit the same crimes time and time again instead.

Is there any hope for you? Will this time be different?

"Insanity is doing the same thing over and over again and expecting different results."
– Albert Einstein

If you want different results, something has to change. Something really big. Let's read the story of a former alcohol and drug addict and jail inmate who met Someone who changed his life. This is a real person and a real story. I changed only the name.

❖ ◆ ❖

My name is Carl Anthony Raines. I started using drugs and drinking at the age of thirteen, with never more than four months of sobriety until two years ago.

My first suicide attempt happened when I turned fifteen; four more were to follow over the next several years. Each time, someone brought me to a hospital psych ward where they watched me until they felt it was safe to send me home. Fourteen times I went through rehab at one place or another, seven were inpatient and seven outpatient. Fourteen times I went right back to drugs and alcohol. Meth was my drug of choice, but I also used cocaine.

I realize now that those fourteen times in rehab failed because they were conducted without God's involvement. That was the key factor. I couldn't do it on my own; I needed His support.

How I made it through high school, I'll never know. I dropped out of all sports and school activities. I ran with the wrong crowds until I became the wrong crowd myself that others ran with. When I graduated, I went to work as a roofer making $1,000 a week.

By the time I was twenty-one, my booze and drug addictions became so out of control that I lost my job, my girlfriend, my dog, and my house. I was in and out of jail four times in two different states, fifty-six days all together. After my last time in county jail, I decided to kill myself by jumping in front of a train the day they let me out. I didn't deserve to live. I had caused so much trouble for my family that I thought they'd be better off without me. I felt the whole world would be better off without me. I was tired of it all.

On the Sunday before my release, I signed up for an afternoon Gideon's presentation. Those are the guys who put Bibles in hotels and motels and conduct Bible studies in jails and other places. Why I signed up, I don't know. I was determined to kill myself in three days. Nothing would stop me from doing that.

One of the two Gideons who talked to five of us that day was a guy named Pat Day. He later told me I looked so hopeless that the Holy Spirit prompted him to ask if I wanted him to mentor me. A mentor is a person who stands alongside of you, like a counselor or coach. Instead of answering him with words, I nodded my head. Why not? At the end of the presentation, he prayed over me and I felt something like hope creep into my bones. I decided to meet with him a time or two before I committed suicide. Maybe he could help me; maybe he couldn't. I thought I'd at least give it a try.

We met at a coffee shop that first time. I brought a Bible along to show him I had some religion in my background. He didn't say much; he mainly listened to my story, writing notes down every once in a while. Before we left, he prayed for me again.

I met with Pat at the same coffee shop one more time. I didn't bring a Bible along. I didn't want to be a phony. I felt God had abandoned me a long time ago because I was such a bad person. How could he love a loser like me? I went through the motions during our time together. This time he did most of the talking, but I wasn't listening much. I had already decided what my next step would be. I don't know why I even met with him.

I had been living with my older sister and her boyfriend. He had gotten a job for me at a manufacturing place nearby, but I quit after three weeks. After my meeting with Pat, I took my car into the woods for a couple of days and various other places for two weeks. I used up what little money I had on meth and booze.

After a couple of days, I needed money to eat and buy drugs. I committed one burglary, a felony, and one theft, a misdemeanor. When that money was gone, I decided now was the time to rid the earth of me. I went to the nearest railroad track and waited for a train to come by. Somehow or another, my sister and my mother found me and brought me to a hospital in Minneapolis.

I had reached my lowest point and decided it was time to turn my life around. I still had Pat's phone number and gave him a call. I told him the whole story of the past two weeks and that I was finally ready to change my behavior for good. He did not criticize me for not making our third meeting, for going off on my own, or even for the two burglaries. He listened to my story until the point when I said, "This time will be different; I'm ready to change."

He told me later that he was planning to encourage me in my decision and offer to help me in whatever way he could. Instead the Holy Spirit guided him to tell me the truth of what would happen to me. I remember it almost word for word.

"No, Carl, you're not going to change your life around. I'll tell you what you're going to do. You're going to leave there in a couple of weeks, and in a matter of days, you're going to be right back where you've always been – on meth and alcohol. You'll need to steal some more to feed your habit. Eventually you'll get caught and thrown in jail again. And then one day, when you can't sink any lower, you're going to try suicide again. This time you may succeed, and you'll spend the rest of eternity in hell. That's what's going to happen to you."

I couldn't believe he told me that; neither could he. In my shell-shocked state, I asked, "What hope is there for me then? What can I do?"

He said matter of factly, "You need to meet the real Jesus. Not the ideas you have about Jesus that you learned in church, but the real Jesus."

I had become a believer at the age of 18 but had walked away from Jesus and wandered around on my own until that evening.

"How do I do that?" I stammered.

"Do you have your own room there?"

"Yes," I answered.

"Do you have a Bible in there?"

'Yes," I answered again.

"Then go into your room, close the door, open your Bible, and ask God to have mercy on your soul and show you who Jesus really is."

I did what he said. What other choice did I have? I prayed, I read the Bible, and then

I prayed and read some more. After what seemed like an hour (it ended up being more than two hours), I experienced Jesus. I didn't see Him in a vision or hear an audible voice, but I knew without a doubt that it was Jesus. It's hard to explain. I felt His presence and then I heard with ears on the inside, not on the outside, a still small voice that said to me, "It will be all right, son."

I felt God's love rain down on me. I cried without tears. My life has not been the same since that day. I entered a Christian rehab place called New Hope Center in Minneapolis and spent 14 months there. During that time, I became grounded in my Christian faith and turned from going my way all the time to going God's way.

I've been to two court hearings for the burglary and the theft. The judge thought I was doing so well that she didn't give me additional jail time. She said when I pay restitution for the thefts and pay my court costs and fees, my two felonies (the other was for possession of meth some time back) will be reduced to misdemeanors. I'm almost there.

I have a full-time job as a fiber optic technician laying high-speed cable to rural homes and businesses. During my time at New Hope, I completed a certificate to be a peer support specialist and hope one day to work in a psych ward, like the last one I was in, to help others like me become sober and stay out of jail.

Through the power of the Holy Spirit, I walked away from jail. I have a new life now, and it's a good one.

❖ ◆ ❖

CHAPTER TWO
The Bad News

RECIDIVISM IS DEFINED AS SOMETHING REPEATED over and over again, as in constantly returning to jail or prison.

At a presentation to a group of men in a county jail in Minnesota, I said, "Some of you have been in jail five times or ten times or maybe even twenty times."

A man in the front row, whose face looked like he'd lost his last friend, spoke up in hopelessness. "Try fifty times."

I could hardly believe it. Fifty times! I'd never heard a number so high before.

The chart on the next page paints the picture of the lives of too many inmates.

You commit a crime. Sometimes you get caught. Sometimes you don't. In this case, you get caught and go to jail or a rehab facility, if you're lucky.

Then comes remorse, which means you're sorry for what you did. "How could I have done this?" you ask yourself. "How could I have been so foolish to get caught?"

Next comes the statement, "I will never go back to jail again. I'm going to turn my life around. This time I can do it." An honest statement, no doubt, but without a serious plan of how to carry it out.

Then you get out of jail or are released from rehab and are free to live your life any way you want. You're grateful to have another chance. You're not going to mess up this time.

But you go back to the same places and the same people and the same stresses in your life. Nothing has really changed. And then, in a moment of weakness or when a serious problem comes up, you revert to your old ways. By and by, you commit the same crime or another just as bad or worse, and you are handcuffed once again and taken to jail.

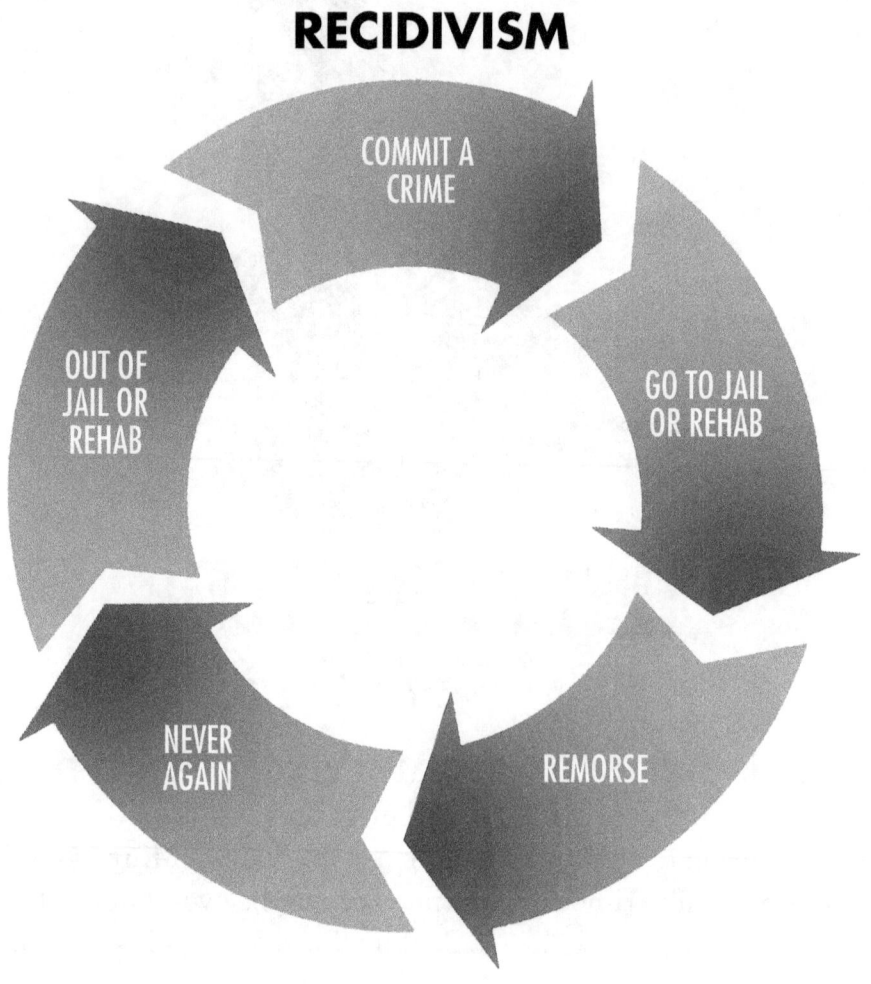

You say you're done making a mess of your life, but you keep doing the same things over and over and over again. It's like watching reruns of a bad movie. One woman in a jail I visited told me she had been clean of drugs for eight years and then one day she ran into a problem she needed to deaden with drugs. And there she was back in jail. When I told a group of inmates in another jail about this, tears came to a man in his 30s as he confessed that he had been sober for ten years and thought he would never go back behind bars, but in a weak moment he slipped.

Bureau of Justice statistics say that 68 % of prisoners released in 30 states were arrested again within three years, and 77 % within five years. Those are 2005 statistics; it might be higher today.

Let's see what the Bible has to say about this problem.

> *But I need something more! For if I know the law but still can't keep it, and if the power of sin within me keeps sabotaging my best intentions, I obviously need help! I realize that I don't have what it takes. I can will it, but I can't do it. I decide to do good, but I don't really do it; I decide not to do bad, but then I do it anyway. My decisions, such as they are, don't result in actions. Something has gone wrong deep within me and gets the better of me every time.*
>
> *It happens so regularly that it's predictable. The moment I decide to do good, sin is there to trip me up. I truly delight in God's commands, but it's pretty obvious that not all of me joins in that delight. Parts of me covertly rebel, and just when I least expect it, they take charge.*
>
> *I've tried everything and nothing helps. I'm at the end of my rope. Is there no one who can do anything for me? Isn't that the real question?*
> – Romans 7:17-24

You look back on your life and see that even your strongest promises to go straight end up in failure. You don't have what it takes to follow through. The world is not fair. The legal system is against you. Your family and friends have betrayed you. What can anyone expect from the conditions you grew up in? It's too much to bear. Can there possibly be any good news for you out there?

Now, here's the thing. To say no to addictions, sex crimes, uncontrolled anger, taking what isn't yours, hanging around with the wrong people, and all the other crimes that land you in jail, there needs to be a greater yes.

For example, if you want to say "No!" to drinking from 4 p.m. until midnight every day, how are you going to fill in those eight hours? You need to have a plan.

> If you just leave a void, you'll eventually go back to the bad habits that sent you to jail in the first place. You can't help yourself. There has to be something else.

> *"Come and let us go up to the mountain of the LORD that He may teach us about His ways and that we may walk in His paths."*
> – Micah 4:2 (NASB)

CHAPTER THREE
The Good News

GOD KNOWS HOW AWFUL YOUR LIFE HAS BEEN. He knows your weakness when you grab for a bottle of liquor or shoot up with drugs to dampen your pain. He knows you have anger issues that can cause you to strike out against others, even those who love you. He knows your bad choices to take what is not yours or to cheat the government or some hapless soul. And yet He does not turn away from you. It is you who have turned away from Him.

    He knows the worst about you, and He loves you just the same.
    There's only One who loves like that, and Jesus is His name.

He can accept a faith that flames out under stress. He takes into account your hidden reasons for failure. He feels the weight of your burdens. That's the God you can trust, the God who knows you like no one else does. You can ask Him for forgiveness, and He won't turn away from you. He is not disappointed in you. He wants the best for you – out of jail and in a loving relationship with Him.

When everyone else has given up on you, He still stands before you with open arms, wanting only to embrace you and tell you that you can be safe if you stay close by Him. No matter how many times you fall, He is always right there to pick you up.

But can you believe that? Can you trust in Him? Let's see what the Bible has to say.

> *Those who enter into Christ's being-here-for-us no longer have to live under a continuous, low-lying black cloud. A new power is in operation. The Spirit of life in Christ, like a strong wind, has magnificently cleared the air, freeing you from a fated lifetime of brutal tyranny at the hands of sin and death.*
>
> *Those who think they can do it on their own end up obsessed with measuring their own moral muscle but never get around to exercising it in real life. Those who trust God's action in them find that God's Spirit is in them—living and breathing God! God leads us out into the open, into a spacious, free life. Focusing on the self is the opposite of focusing on God.*
>
> *So don't you see that we don't owe this old do-it-yourself life one red cent. There's nothing in it for us, nothing at all. The best thing to do is give it a decent burial and get on with your new life. God's Spirit beckons. There are things to do and places to go! – Romans 8:5-18*

Don't you see, the strength you need to stay away from crime is not in yourself. It never was and never will be.

> You keep looking in all the wrong places for meaning – a girlfriend or boyfriend, a spouse, a gang, a job, a new location far away from where you got into trouble.

But these are not reliable or steady. They all can change like the flip of a coin. You need an anchor bigger than yourself or someone else or something else. Jesus Christ is that anchor you can depend on when life is filled with trouble and anxiety and unpredictability. Let's turn to the Bible again.

> *Don't be obsessed with getting more material things. Be relaxed with what you have. Since God assured us, "I'll never let you down, never walk off and leave you," we can boldly quote,*

God is there, ready to help;
I'm fearless no matter what.
Who or what can get to me?

There should be a consistency that runs through us all. For Jesus doesn't change—yesterday, today, tomorrow, he's always totally himself.
– Hebrews 13:5-8

Some of you may be born-again Christians who have strayed away from Jesus. Some of you may not be born-again yet. What is this born-again stuff? It's not complicated.

Ask yourself, "Who or what can get to me other than God?" The answer to that question is who or what you have put in the place of God. Is it money you want or a fancy car? Is it something that someone else has? Is it drugs or alcohol or pornography or games you play on electronic devices? Is it belonging to a group of like-minded wrongdoers? Is it demanding your rights? Is it someone who has done you wrong and you need to get back at them? Is it a probation that is too strict or the impulse to drive a vehicle when you're high?

All these things are the product of being born into the sinful condition of Adam and Eve. It's all you can expect in the natural world. You can't turn your back on it or outrun it. You can't bury it once and for all. You need to be born-again into the spiritual world, into God's world. It's your best hope of staying out of jail. It's the only way to become the person God wants you to be – His son or daughter, safe in His arms.

❖ ◆ ❖

There is a CHOICE to be made!

We are first born into a natural life with Adam and Eve as the representatives of the human race. When we choose Jesus Christ to be our representative instead, we are born-again into a spiritual relationship with Him.

HOPING TO MAKE IT TO HEAVEN BY LIVING A GOOD LIFE will not get you there. Knowing what it takes to be saved won't get you there, nor will going to church or talking a good game. Being baptized as a baby is a dedication of you by your parents, but it's not a choice you made. And there needs to be a choice on your part, a choice to give up your life of sin and self-sufficiency and accept Jesus as your Savior and your Lord. He died on the cross for your sins, but just knowing that and believing He has a wonderful gift waiting for you is not enough. You have to take the gift by an act of your will.

It's like being very, very hungry and a great banquet is spread out before you. But all the food doesn't do you a lick of good unless you take it and eat it. If you only look at it, you will eventually die of starvation.

Or maybe you're stricken with cancer and told it can be easily cured with one radiation treatment, but until you choose to allow the treatment, your cancer remains and you'll eventually die.

That's the way it is with Jesus. The original sin of Adam and Eve and your own sins are a cancer that brings death to your spirit. Jesus Christ is the treatment to bring life to your spirit forever, to make you a new person. His death on the cross is a gift of grace to bring you to salvation, so you can be born again from your natural world of sin to the spiritual world of life with Christ.

> Grace means something you didn't earn or deserve, but it's given to you anyway because of God's love for you. There's only one catch. Like any other gift, the gift of grace can be yours only if you'll reach out and take it.

Think of it this way. The American evangelist D.L. Moody was once walking along the banks of the muddy Chicago River, contemplating how salvation works. In the distance, ahead of him, he saw a small group gathered in a circle, looking down at the ground. As he approached, he saw a man lying on his stomach in the middle of the group. Someone was kneeling in front of him, pressing on the man's upper body, trying to resuscitate him. Moody looked at this man who had just been pulled from the river and saw dirty water running out of his nose, mouth, and ears.

Instantly it became a picture of the issue he had been contemplating. In salvation a person is pulled from the river of death and the "dirty water" (sin) is expelled and life-giving "oxygen" (the Holy Spirit) streams in to replace it.

Let's take a look at how this all works in real life.

IN THE BEGINNING ADAM AND EVE HAD A DIRECT CONNECTION TO GOD. They walked with Him and talked with Him in the Garden of Eden. His Spirit lived within their spirit. They had safety and peace and all they needed every day. It's how God meant it to be. All God asked of them was to stay connected to Him in obedience and love. God gave them a free will to choose wisely, but they chose foolishly instead, and sin came into the world.

ADAM AND EVE BROKE THAT CONNECTION when they exercised their free will and disobeyed their Creator by eating fruit from the Tree of the Knowledge of Good and Evil, in direct disobedience to God's command. It was as if they shook their fists at God and said they wanted to be gods themselves, to go their own way, just like Satan had done. Instead of communing with God, they communed with Satan, and took down the whole human race with them, separating all of us from a direct connection to God from birth.

WE ARE BORN SINFUL because our great…great…great grandfather Adam and our great…great…great grandmother Eve, our original ancestors, rebelled against God and chose to go their own way. We are born into that original sin and add on plenty more of our own. In short, we're tainted with sin when we come out of the womb. It's who we are, all of us.

Because of the creation of Adam and Eve, we are born with two eyes, two ears, two arms, and two lungs, and we have one nose, one mouth, one heart, and one liver. Because of them, we can walk, talk, and think. We inherit everything from them, including our sinful nature. It's in our makeup, deep within us.

Men and women have tried to reconnect to God ever since the fall of Adam and Eve. Some by going to church. Some by making sincere vows. Some by doing good, but whatever they do, it's not good enough. It is hopeless; we are doomed to eternal separation from God. There is no way we can bridge the gap on our own. Every man and woman falls short of the glory of God, dead in their sins.

BUT GOD HAS A WONDERFUL PLAN FOR US. Though we can't bridge the gap, God has done it for us. Jesus Christ came to earth—God in the form of man—to take the penalty of our sins. It is His death and resurrection that bridges the gap between God and man. And so we can reconnect to eternal life with God—what Adam and Eve had lost—through the cross of Jesus. Hallelujah, you can be saved or re-establish a close relationship with Jesus again if you have been saved.

NO ONE COMES TO THE FATHER EXCEPT THROUGH JESUS. He tells us in John 14 that He is the Way and the Truth and the Life. If you could do anything to earn your way into heaven, there would have been no reason for the Father to send His Son Jesus to die for your sins. There is a debt to be paid for your sinful nature and the many sins you have committed, and you don't have the wherewithal to pay it. But Jesus paid it for you on the cross.

LET'S SAY YOU COME BEFORE A JUDGE in a courtroom for a brutal murder you have committed. You would never have done something like that except you were so high on drugs and alcohol that you didn't know what you were doing. You don't even remember stabbing your best friend over and over and over again.

You are ashamed of what you did and say how sorry you are. But the judge has to do what he has to do. He sentences you to death by lethal injection. As you are being led out of the courtroom in handcuffs to the fate you deserve, he says, "Wait. Let him go free. I will take his place instead."

But so far those are only words. You have to accept his offer and physically change places with him. You hold your hands out to the guards and they take off your cuffs. Then you step away from the guards and let the judge take your place to be executed instead of you. It's always a choice.

That judge is Jesus Christ, and He has died for the sin you inherited from Adam and Eve and all the sins you have committed against Him, your fellow travelers on this earth, and society as a whole. You walk out of that courtroom a new person. The old has gone away. The new has come. Praise God for His mercy on you.

BACK TO THE CHOICE YOU HAVE TO MAKE. So far, we have been talking concepts. Now it's time to put salvation into practice with three choices, what I call the ABCs of salvation.

> A. **Will you ADMIT** you have a sinful nature from the day you were born and have sinned against God again and again and again? **Will you ADMIT** you are a failure when it comes to earning your way into heaven? **Will you ADMIT** your natural self in Adam is hopelessly corrupt and needs redemption?
>
> B. **Do you BELIEVE** what Jesus says about Himself in Scripture – that He is the Way and the Truth and the Life and that no one comes to the Father except through Him? **Do you BELIEVE** He died on the cross for your sins and is waiting for you to come to him? **Do you BELIEVE** the Holy Spirit will come live in your spirit when you are born-again and show you how to live a spiritual life?
>
> C. **Will you CHOOSE** Jesus Christ as your Savior and ask Him to come into your life for all eternity? **Will you CHOOSE** Him also as your Lord and follow Him with all your heart and with all your soul? **Will you CHOOSE** to step from the left side of the cross in the last illustration and walk over to the other side, in humble submission to the One who loves you so much that He died for you?

If you have chosen to receive Jesus into your heart, then you have the Holy Spirit living inside you, and the rest of this book will make sense to you. If you are already a born-again Christian, you can rededicate your life to Jesus and have a deeper personal relationship with Him so earnest that you won't go your own way again.

If you are of a different religion than Christianity or if you don't choose to be born-again at this time, you can still open your heart to God's assistance. You can choose to follow His commands and His ways in your life and stop going your own way. I cannot speak to those who have no God in their lives other than to say, "You need Him."

❖ ◆ ❖

CHAPTER FOUR
The Melody of the Holy Spirit

LET'S FACE IT. We live in a secular world where anything goes – alcohol, drugs, sex, greed, anger, hatred, and more sins than can be named. One in ten Americans over the age of 12 is addicted to drugs and alcohol. That's roughly the size of Texas. Let's look at what Romans 1:18-23 has to say about this.

> *What happened was this: People knew God perfectly well, but when they didn't treat him like God, refusing to worship him, they trivialized themselves into silliness and confusion so that there was neither sense nor direction left in their lives. They pretended to know it all, but were illiterate regarding life. They traded the glory of God who holds the whole world in his hands for... rampant evil... [and] keep inventing new ways of wrecking lives.*

We're talking both Christians and non-Christians here. Even if you have been born-again from your natural sinful state at birth into a new spiritual state – from the natural world into the spiritual world – you still have those natural tendencies tempting you. They don't just go away in a flash, at least not for most people. If you craved alcohol and drugs before being saved, the craving will still be there after. There are exceptions, miracles so to speak, but you will most likely struggle with addiction until you close the gap between you and Jesus. The same goes with anger issues and stealing and all the other things that get you in trouble with the law. They are like magnets that draw you into committing the same crimes over and over again, whether you are a Christian or not.

> Your life without Jesus is like swimming too near a rip tide. One wrong move and you're swept out to sea.

First of all, there is the sad state of the world. You can buy drugs on any street corner. Alcohol is legal to buy no matter what your condition. Nasty people rub you the wrong way. Even your best friends can turn on you at any minute. You may have been abused as a child or lived in a dysfunctional family. You may have grown up in the wrong part of town.

> For the most part, the world is not your friend.

Then there is the sinful and self-centered you. In your natural state, you stand at the front of the stage and see everyone else as supporting actors. You make friends based on what others can do for you. You find boyfriends or girlfriends that satisfy your needs. You become upset when others don't respect your rights. You strike out when anger gets the best of you. You live for your own pleasure and your own satisfaction, taking up drugs and alcohol to make you feel good. Only when the law gets in your way do you suffer consequences for your actions – and the law always seems to get in the way for you.

I'm using the word you, but I have the same natural tendency to stand at the front of the stage and do things that are favorable for me, that make me feel good, and that satisfy my own needs even if they are unhelpful to others. I fight that all the time.

> We need something solid underneath us. We need some way to experience God when the music of the world blares away at us and the song of ourselves plays loudly.

That something is what I call the under melody of the Holy Spirit. I'm going to take an excerpt from my book called Arm in Arm with the Holy Spirit to tell you what I mean in story form. In this part of the story, I'm in a church service in Fargo, North Dakota, with my mother.

> Pastor Lee's sermon was titled The Unter Melody (unter being the German word for under). Here's what he said: "Underneath the song of this world, filled with family, friends, food, jobs, and everyday events, plays the subtle melody of the Holy Spirit; and if we desire with all our heart to stay near Jesus, that melody should fill our mind, will, and emotions every waking hour."
>
> As I left the church arm in arm with my mother, I was also arm in arm with the Holy Spirit.

This is really the only safe place to be for you – walking arm in arm with the Holy Spirit, listening to His melody instead of the music of the world and the song of your own self. Picture yourself walking through life alongside Jesus, seeing the world as He sees it, listening to His voice deep within you as you make choices both big and small. But how do you hear His melody with all the noise in your life? Let's turn to another passage in my book to grasp the idea of listening for the under melody by seeing how it works in church music. I'm at Life 21 Church in Northfield, Minnesota.

> The service started with praise and worship music. The worship team's final song was Jesus, Lover of my soul; Jesus, I will never let You go. It was gently reaching its conclusion when the lead guitarist, a young woman named Libby, began softly playing a different melody with different words, marvelous and almost supernatural. The new melody seemed to float underneath the main melody so subtly I could barely hear it at first. The volume of this under melody gradually increased until I could hear the music and her words more clearly.
>
> Gradually, the other musicians shifted to the melody Libby was playing and the phrases she was singing, adding praise and worship words of their own. This under melody, which was now the only melody, continued for at least ten minutes. The congregation, including me, was greatly affected. Some stood in the aisles with heads bowed, many fell to their knees, and a few came forward and lay prostrate before the altar. I sat with head in hands, overwhelmed by it all.
>
> After the service, I approached Libby and asked if the worship team practiced the last song the way it unfolded. She smiled and said, "No." A nudge from within prompted a follow-up question: "Was it the Holy Spirit who directed you to play the new song?" She smiled again and said, "Yes."

Can you see the metaphor, the comparison of this under melody to your own life? The music of the world and your own self-centered ways are always playing in your life, just as they are always playing in my life. But underneath that main music is the under melody of the Holy Spirit that plays the gentle song of Jesus Christ and His Father. The theme of that song is so different from the blare of the world and your own noisy doings.

It's beautiful beyond description.

> If you put yourself in places where this under melody plays and listen carefully for it, you will hear God speaking to you.

It might be when you're reading the Bible or praying through the power of the Holy Spirit. Or in a Bible study or fellowship with a like-minded believer. When you are serving someone else instead of yourself, you will hear it. Or in a Spirit-filled church service where people submit themselves in praise and worship.

> An inmate named Shirley could only hear the music of drugs, stealing, and striking back at those who didn't let her do what she wanted to do. She was in and out of jail for thirteen years. One day, when she was out of jail but a step away from heading back in, a friend told her about Jesus. By this time, Shirley realized that no matter what she did, she could not stay out of jail. She just couldn't help herself. She was at the end of her rope. When she accepted Jesus as her Savior and Lord, for the first time she had hope that she could stay out of jail.
> But, oh, the song of drugs and a life filled with pleasure played so strongly that she told her friend she didn't know how much longer she could hold out. The friend finally persuaded her to sign up for the thirteen-month program at the Adult and Teen Challenge women's facility in Minneapolis. From the day she entered the front door, she listened to the melody of the Holy Spirit from the time she got up in the morning until the time she went to bed at night – Christian teaching, one-on-one counseling, study groups, singing praise and worship music, fellowship with believers, devouring the Bible, praying continually. That's what she heard every day, so loudly that she no longer heard the music of the world and her own self-centered self.

You see, even after Shirley became a Christian, she still couldn't get rid of the temptations in her soul. She needed a firm foundation of Christian living to strengthen her resolve and bolster her sinful nature to resist drugs.

Does everyone need to go into a thirteen-month program? I'm not saying that. Shirley did. You may not. But, you do need to get into a routine where you hear the under melody of the Holy Spirit on a regular basis.

❖ ◆ ❖

CHAPTER FIVE
The Radio Dial Metaphor

THE BOOK *ARM IN ARM WITH THE HOLY SPIRIT* has major metaphors (one thing standing for another) that show how important it is to stay near the Holy Spirit. This one took place in the same church in Northfield.

All services I attended at Life 21 began the same way: personal testimonies followed by praise and worship music. This day was different. Pastor Lew walked in slow motion up the middle aisle and stood quietly before the altar for at least a minute. No one knew what was about to happen, not even Pastor Lew. As he had once said to the congregation, "I don't run this service; the Holy Spirit does."

He turned to face the congregation and requested in a soft voice I'd never heard him use before: "For those who can, please go to your knees and silently pray to forget yourselves and the things of this world and prepare to worship the living God." That's all he said.

I knelt and began to pray mindlessly: "Lord, I ask that You help me forget about myself and the things of this world," and continued on in that fashion. The Holy Spirit was not impressed with such a lifeless prayer and turned my mind to an inward vision. In my imagination, I saw a radio with a manual-tuning dial and an FM broadcast frequency band that had stations on either end, like the image at the beginning of this chapter.

The station at 107.9 FM played the Holy Spirit Station loud and clear, with a gentle melody that spoke of God's values and his love for me. The station at 87.7 FM played the World/Self Station loud and clear, blasting out the values of the world and blaring at me to do things my way.

The signal of the Holy Spirit Station can be heard along the entire frequency band, but the strength of its signal is strongest the closer a believer is tuned toward 107.9 and weakest the nearer 87.7. In the same way, the signal of the World/Self Station can be heard along the entire frequency band, but the strength of its signal is strongest the closer one is tuned toward 87.7 and weakest the nearer 107.9. The music of the world/self is always present within a believer, and so too the melody of the Holy Spirit. The place where the two signals are of equal strength is 97.9.

When I realized my prayer had taken place somewhere in the middle frequencies, I turned the dial to a higher frequency. It was so real I could see my hand turning the frequency knob. Then I repented of my having wandered away from the Lord that morning and prayed to remain close to Jesus the rest of the day. I felt that was a prayer He would honor, and He did. The congregation remained in silent prayer for five minutes; then the testimonies began.

Do you see it? There are two choices ever before us. Do we tune to the World/Self Station and hear a little interference from the Holy Spirit Station? Or do we tune to the melody of the Holy Spirit with a trace of static from the World/Self frequency?

We can barely hear the voice of God when we're focused on ourselves and the things of this world. We can hear Him clearly and distinctly when we're in tune with the Holy Spirit.

Let me tell you how this plays out for me. I'm tuned into the Holy Spirit Station when I'm speaking to inmates in county jails or at rehab centers like Adult and Teen Challenge. I'm in the higher frequencies when I'm reading the Bible or spending time in prayer or being focused on the Lord in a church or Bible study.

The same things work for you when you hang around in the same places where the

Holy Spirit hangs around – with other inmates who are Christians, in Sunday worship time and Gideon Bible studies, reading your Bible, praying that the Holy Spirit will keep you close to Jesus, witnessing to those who are lost, being an encourager to those who are ready to give up.

If you want to go to a movie, you go to a movie house. If you want to bowl, you go to a bowling alley. It's the same thing with walking arm in arm with the Holy Spirit. You need to be in places where He lives – the places named above for example. You can figure out other places.

But here's the thing, if you're not purposely staying near the Holy Spirit Station, you gradually drift back to the World/Self Station. It's the way it goes. And the closer you get to that station, the less you hear the godly station. And that's where you get into trouble and go back to your old ways. You are not safe anywhere below 97.9 FM, where the music of the world and your own self-centered self is louder than the melody of the Holy Spirit. When there is more of your music and less of the melody of the Holy Spirit, you are in a place where you may soon be heading back to jail. When there is more of the melody of the Holy Spirit than your music, you are in a place where you can resist temptation through the power of the Holy Spirit.

> It's all about choices. You choose where to live your life, near God or near yourself. You either do it God's way or you do it your way. The one will keep you out of jail; the other won't. Your way doesn't work, but I don't need to tell you that. You have a track record of making the wrong choices and suffering the consequences. You can't help yourself, but God can help you if you let Him. You've been going your own direction for too long, and it's been hopeless. Try turning around 180 degrees and going in God's direction.

But it's not a one-time thing. It's like weeding a garden. You don't just pull all the weeds out once and think they'll never come back. They always do. You need to pull out the weeds on a daily basis and water the plants often to have a healthy garden. It's the same way with your life. You need to pull out the constant temptations from Satan and water your soul with the life-giving water of the Holy Spirit. When you don't nurture the garden of your soul, the temptations take over and your whole life goes into disrepair, and another sentence to jail is just around the corner.

❖ ◆ ❖

CHAPTER SIX
The Mobile Bay Estuary Metaphor

THE SECOND MAJOR METAPHOR OF MY BOOK answers the two questions I often ask in my presentations and visits to the Wright County Jail for Gideon Bible studies on Sunday afternoons.

The first question is this: "How many of you were born-again Christians when you committed your last crime?" Many hands go up.

Then I ask: "How's it possible that you were saved from your sins and then went right back to do the same crimes or worse?" I get mostly blank looks. Then I show them the metaphor of Mobile Bay. It's when you are so far away from God that you are in danger of repeating the same behavior.

Mobile Bay is the fourth largest estuary in the United States. An estuary is when a coastal body of fresh water has an open connection with a body of salt water, such as the Mobile, Tensaw, and a few other rivers emptying into the northern reaches of Mobile Bay.

The salt water represents the world and your all-about-me self. The fresh water represents the Holy Spirit. Notice on the illustration that the northern half of the estuary has a higher concentration of fresh water, shown by the lines being closer together – meaning, more of the Holy Spirit. The southern half has more salt water, shown by the lines being farther apart – meaning less of the Holy Spirit and more of the world and your natural self.

Where the compass needle intersects Mobile Bay is where the fresh water and salt water is equal; that is, you are half full of God and half full of the world and yourself.

Now here's the thing. When you are more filled with God than yourself, above the compass point, you are safe. You're in God's world. He wants what's best for you, and that doesn't include going back to jail. He is your strength and He will help you stay out of jail. The northern part of Mobile Bay is where you are close to God and you can hear Him speak into your heart through Bible Study, prayer, meditation, and other ways of listening for His voice and seeing Him in action.

When you are more filled with the world and yourself than God, below the compass point, you are in danger. You're living in the natural world with Adam and Eve as your rulers. You're going your own way, and your own way is what sends you back to jail. The farther south you drift, the less you can hear His voice or even know He's around. It's the place where you do the very things that land you back in jail.

The whole of Mobile Bay is the territory of a born-again Christian. Within the bay, believers are going to heaven. Below the bay and into the Gulf of Mexico, non-believers have another destination waiting for them.

There is a big difference between being saved (within Mobile Bay) and being a disciple of Jesus Christ (in the northern half). Being saved sends you to heaven, but it doesn't keep you out of jail. That's why even those of you who are born-again end up doing the same crimes over and over again. It's when you're following your own sinful inclinations and the ways of the world, when you're not following Jesus with all your heart and with all your soul, that you may be going to heaven, but you're living a miserable life here on earth (in the southern half).

If you're a disciple, you give up everything to follow Jesus. You are more concerned with pleasing Him than in pleasing yourself and others. You ask Him, "What should I do here, Lord?"

You promise, "I will put all my faith in You, Jesus, and no faith in myself.

> I have tried and tried again to stop doing the things that get me in trouble, but it doesn't work. I give up! I will follow You to the ends of the earth. I will obey Your commands. I will look at the world through Your eyes. I will follow Your teachings by reading Your Word. I will pray continually through the power of the Holy Spirit. I will walk arm in arm with the Holy Spirit. I will depend on His guidance and His teaching me how to live out my Christian life. I will seek out God-fearing men and women of faith to be my friends. From this day forth, Lord, You will be my number one priority."

All of us have two selves – the natural one and the spiritual one. We are born into the natural world, and Adam and Eve are our great…great…great grandparents. Like them, we have two each of eyes, ears, hands, feet, kidneys, and lungs. We have a nose, a mouth, a heart, an appendix, and a pancreas. And we inherit their disobedience and rebellion against God when they chose to go their own way in the Garden of Eden. It is called original sin or ancestral sin. It's in our genes, as surely as we have two lungs and a heart.

God told both of them they would die if they ate of the fruit of the forbidden tree. First would come spiritual death. Eventually there would be physical death, which was not in God's original plan. The connection between them and Him was broken, and we are born into that broken condition. And, of course, we pile on thousands of sins of our own to that sinful nature. That's what Romans 7 is all about.

Accepting that Jesus died on the cross to re-establish that connection and accepting Him as the spiritual head of the human race and as our Savior and Lord puts us firmly in the world of a personal relationship with Jesus Christ and His Father, through the power of the Holy Spirit. It's a one-time commitment but we need to be constantly working out that salvation.

We choose moment by moment to do things our way or God's way. We either accept the natural way of Adam or the spiritual way of Jesus Christ. Now, here is a very important point: if we do nothing, we default to our way, the natural way, Adam's way. It's like always turning on a TV to the same channel. To get a different channel, you have to make a choice. It's that way with living in God's world. We have to intend to go there; we have to be persistent to stay there; we have to be very careful not to slip back into the natural world and doing things our way.

> If the Lord is huge and can beat any of your problems, why don't you find His will in your life? Invite Him into the fight. He is bigger than whatever you are facing in this world. He knows all the bad things you have done and still believes in your potential. You may feel like a loser because you're in jail, but God sees you as a mighty warrior and a hero in His kingdom. Whose team do you want to be on – the World/Self losers or the Holy Spirit winners?

❖ ◆ ❖

CHAPTER SEVEN
The Good Shepherd

We're all like sheep who've wandered off and gotten lost. We've all done our own thing, gone our own way. And GOD has piled all our sins, everything we've done wrong, on him. – Isaiah 53:6

YOU MAKE THE SAME MISTAKES OVER AND OVER, hoping that somehow everything will turn out right in the end. You keep doing the same things but expect different results. Perhaps happiness is just around the next corner or on the other side of the upcoming hill. Yet, it's not there. You're looking for happiness in all the wrong places.

Now and then you set out to restore yourself, saying, "This time I'll deal with my addictions, my anger, my stealing, or [whatever your crime is]." Maybe you will. Maybe you won't, and the cycle continues. Despite your promises to end your sinful ways once and for all, nothing long-lasting happens. You go back to your old ways.

You may blame bad genes, your dysfunctional family, the poverty you grew up in, a series of lousy friends, the legal system that hounds you, and a hundred other problems. But no one had to push you into wrongdoing. You did that all by yourself.

Though you are stubborn and rebellious, Jesus, the Good Shepherd, will never give up pursuing you. He can't get you off His mind. He knows well your condition. He sees the look of hopelessness on each face. He knows every insult you have suffered. He knows people have hurt you and led you astray. He knows when you have been abused and misused, the wounds others have given you, and the sin of your own rebellion. Psalm 147:2-6 speaks to us about God's mercy.

> *He heals the heartbroken*
> *and bandages their wounds.*
> *He counts the stars*
> *and assigns each a name.*
> *Our Lord is great, with limitless strength;*
> *we'll never comprehend what he knows and does.*
> *GOD puts the fallen on their feet again.*

He says, "I will bind up the injured and strengthen the weak." He has compassion on those who have been set back by their own sin. He understands sorrow, misfortune, broken homes, and shattered dreams.

Jesus has laid down His life for His sheep, of which you are one. He waits for you to come back from your wandering ways and become one of the sheep of his flock, protected from the wilderness and prowling wolves. He is the Father who welcomes back his prodigal son in Luke 15:11-32.

> *There was once a man who had two sons. The younger said to his father, "Father, I want right now what's coming to me."*
>
> *So the father divided the property between them. It wasn't long before the younger son packed his bags and left for a distant country. There, undisciplined and dissipated, he wasted everything he had. After he had gone through all his money, there was a bad famine all through that country and he began to hurt. He signed on with a citizen there who assigned him to his fields to slop the pigs. He was so hungry he would have eaten the corncobs in the pig slop, but no one would give him any.*
>
> *That brought him to his senses. He said, "All those farmhands working for my father sit down to three meals a day, and here I am starving to death. I'm going back to my father. I'll say to him, Father, I've sinned against God, I've sinned before you; I don't deserve to be*

called your son. Take me on as a hired hand." He got right up and went home to his father.

When he was still a long way off, his father saw him. His heart pounding, he ran out, embraced him, and kissed him. The son started his speech: "Father, I've sinned against God, I've sinned before you; I don't deserve to be called your son ever again."

But the father wasn't listening. He was calling to the servants, "Quick. Bring a clean set of clothes and dress him. Put the family ring on his finger and sandals on his feet. Then get a grain-fed heifer and roast it. We're going to feast! We're going to have a wonderful time! My son is here—given up for dead and now alive! Given up for lost and now found!" And they began to have a wonderful time.

You see, Jesus came to seek and to save those who have been lost, of which you are one. He wants all the lost sheep to come to his sheep pen, no matter how wayward or bedraggled. Can you not hear Him calling for you to come back? Will you not listen to Him as He searches high and low for you, whispering your name and inviting you to come follow Him?

He will lead you to safety and will be your Shepherd. You may be on a cold mountain or in a dense forest with wild animals waiting to devour you. Call out to Him, and He will come to your rescue.

The Good Shepherd lays down His life for His sheep. Oh, lost sheep, let Him find you waiting for Him. Let Him comfort you and sustain you. Let Him rescue you and bring you back to His flock. Listen to His voice as He says, "I am the Good Shepherd. I lay down my life for my sheep. All I ask is that you heed my voice and come to me and follow me and let me lead you for the rest of your life."

Let Him bring you back to His flock that lives in safety. Be able to say as David did in Psalm 23.

GOD is my shepherd!
I don't need a thing.
You have bedded me down in lush meadows,
you find me quiet pools to drink from.
True to your word,
you let me catch my breath
and send me in the right direction.
Even when the way goes through
Death Valley,

*I'm not afraid
when you walk at my side.
Your trusty shepherd's crook
makes me feel secure.
You serve me a six-course dinner
right in front of my enemies.
You revive my drooping head;
my cup brims with blessing.
Your beauty and love chase after me
every day of my life.
I'm back home in the house of GOD
for the rest of my life.*

Doesn't this sound good? Instead of wandering around in thickets and brambles and rocky places, you can lie down in green pastures and drink cool water. Even when you encounter dark places in life, He is right by your side.

Though others may give up on you, the Lord never will. You need not be lonely and afraid ever again. He will never give up looking for you. Right now He is inviting you back to the safety of His flock. Will you follow Him wherever He goes? He will lead, but you must choose to follow. It's always a choice!

God's presence does not reside in your intellect but in your heart. Your mind is fed by the world and all your thoughts about yourself. It's the outer you. Your heart is the inner you, made up of your desires, values, loves, and will. It's where your conscience lies. When you invite Christ into your life, it's not into your mind but into your heart. And then your heart feeds your mind.

❖ ◆ ❖

CHAPTER EIGHT
The King's Highway and Lake Calhoun

IN THE BOOK I WROTE CALLED *ARM IN ARM WITH THE HOLY SPIRIT*, I recorded a vision I had years back that had to do with following Jesus every step of the way.

> While driving to Minneapolis yesterday, I envisioned a road of a much different nature running parallel to the highway I was on.
>
> In a flash, I was walking on the other road, a path of smooth gravel, winding through woods and open spaces, with Christ ahead of me. He turned and spoke almost in a whisper, "Patrick, come follow Me."
>
> I said, "Yes, Lord."
>
> He continued the conversation, "Do you see any need to pile up money for retirement?"
>
> I replied, "No, Lord."
>
> "Do you see any need for a new house, fashionable clothes, or a

shiny new car?"

"No, my Lord."

"Are there any needs you have on this road?"

"None," I answered. "To be with You is all I want. You will provide everything I need." With this confession, I experienced a feeling of great peace.

Alongside the road were wild animals and monsters, but I knew they couldn't harm me because I was with the King. As we were about to enter a dense woods, I had a strong urge to turn around and go back a few hundred yards.

"Lord, I wish to see for just a minute what I have left behind." I returned to an opening in the woods and noticed the path I was on with Jesus stood above a deep ditch with steep sides. The ditch was filled with various distorted figures personifying greed, envy, gossip, pleasure, dishonesty, immorality, alcoholism, and the other things of this world not part of the King's neighborhood. I also saw some real people, though I couldn't recognize anyone in particular.

"Come down with us," the misshapen figures and people shouted. "Life is good here. Don't be a Goody Two-Shoes. A life of pleasure is the best life of all. This is where you'll find happiness." But they didn't look happy, and a miry sludge lapped at their heels. I realized their lot in life was to slide back into that sludge, the whole dirty, tattered, and earthy lot of them. Yet, the ditch and what was in it tempted me.

Jesus showed up at that point and sighed, "Patrick, come follow Me." Those in the ditch couldn't see Him. I realized if I crawled down into the ditch, I also would not be able to see Him. Eventually, I would forget Him, and the miry sludge would be lapping at my heels.

"Come, follow Me," Jesus repeated.

"Yes, Lord, I will follow You."

Those in the ditch heard the exchange and yelled, "You fool!" but they had no attraction for me anymore.

I was on the high road with my Lord, and that's where I desired to be. Psalm 73:25-28 resonated in my mind:

You're all I want in heaven!
You're all I want on earth!
When my skin sags and my bones get brittle,
GOD is rock-firm and faithful.
Look! Those who left you are falling apart!
Deserters, they'll never be heard from again.
But I'm in the very presence of GOD —

Oh, how refreshing it is!
I've made Lord GOD my home.
GOD, I'm telling the world what you do!

How does this vision apply to you? Don't you see it? You're the one who goes back on the path to see the world you came from, a deep ditch with steep sides. The ditch is filled with the people and places of your criminal past. Drug pushers, fellow heavy drinkers, thieves, liars, gang members, and dishonorable people of every stripe. They want you to come back and live with them. Then there are the bars, parties, homes and businesses to be broken into, cars to be driven while high on drugs and alcohol, government agencies to be defrauded, probation to be violated, and all sorts of settings for you to take advantage of others for your own gain.

Who are you going to listen to? The people and places of your past, or Jesus who is leading you on a straight and safe road? It's a choice at every turn. It's always a choice. If you don't choose to follow alongside Jesus, you're on your own, and you already know where that takes you. Stay out of the ditches of life. Stay on the King's Highway.

Don't let your spiritual life get cold. Here's what happened to me when I let my busy life get in the way of following Jesus on His path. I went my own way, and my own way usually led to trouble someplace down the line, as it does for you. This is a passage from my book. If I had been addicted to drugs or alcohol or pornography, I would have been in danger of a relapse.

> During this season of bitterness and infighting at the college, I put my relationship with God on the back burner, as I tried to keep the pots on the front burners from boiling over. It was like juggling tigers, one mistake and they'd eat me alive. I drove to work at the crack of dawn instead of spending an hour in prayer, worship, and reading Scripture. I was too busy during the day to pray or keep the Lord in mind. My assistant said to me, "Pat, if you keep up this pace of activity, you're going to keel over. If I could help more than I am, I would. But I don't want to collapse either."
>
> God could have smoothed the way had I asked Him. But it was all me, me, me, and it, it, it. My hair was shaggy and my beard scruffy because I didn't have time for a cut and trim. My wife laid out my clothes each night so I didn't have to do it in the morning.
>
> Exhaustion followed me home every night. I only had the energy to eat, watch an hour of TV, and go to bed early. My kids asked why I acted as if they were not there, and my wife was disheartened by the manner in which I was conducting myself. I felt guilty, but what could I do? There was a college to save.
>
> I also ignored the Holy Spirit; and the farther I distanced myself from Him, the less I recognized it. I had once asked Him to let me know when I was drifting so far from God I couldn't feel His presence. He chose the

venue of a softball field just west of Lake Calhoun in Minneapolis to teach me a lesson from God's classroom.

I'd started running during the summer of my twenty-second year when it wasn't yet fashionable to loop around a quarter-mile track four times without being in some sort of race. Running exhilarated me and became a lifetime habit, eventually evolving into a regular jog of three miles, five times a week. My favorite running setting of all time was the three-mile path around Lake Calhoun. It was a popular walking, running, and biking site at the time, and still is.

I was a gregarious fellow by nature and in the habit of starting up conversations with people I'd never met or even seen before. It might be, for example, a person standing behind me in a grocery check-out line, or a stranger running around Lake Calhoun at about my speed. I'd run up behind him and ask, "How are you doing?" And he'd answer that he was running to clear his head for a new job he'd be starting the next day. Two miles later, I knew about the work he did, the family he had, and the church he attended.

A large softball field, which doubled as a soccer and lacrosse area, sat on the west side of Lake Calhoun, and it's where I always ended up after a run, walking across the outfield and the infield to an aluminum bench on the first-base side. There I'd sit and rest up from the run.

August 6, 1989, was a torrid summer day, at the same time my spiritual life was in the refrigerator, placed there by me as I dealt with the turmoil of the college. For the previous four months, I rarely opened the refrigerator door. I don't think I even knew where it was most of the time. I'd strayed far enough from Jesus that I was in danger of not knowing how to find my way back. I was not lost from my salvation but my working it out was absent without leave.

I'd just finished a college meeting in St. Paul and thirty minutes later was changing into running clothes at my usual parking spot by the field, hoping no one would walk by and see what I was doing. I was especially nervous about taking my pants off and putting on running shorts. I was afraid a cop would drive by and arrest me for indecent exposure.

The weather was tropical, near one-hundred degrees; and the humidity was so steamy a lake fog shimmered over Calhoun, giving the water a surreal look. I was the only one on the running path. Many times I wanted to stop but plodded on. My running rules dictated that if I stopped to rest, the run wouldn't count. So I jogged on deliberately, step after weary step, the sweat on my face nearly blinding me. The only thing that kept me going was the thought of the bench at the end of the run. After running for what seemed like a week, and staggering across left field, I plopped down on the bench, exhausted in body, mind, emotions, and will. It was the perfect classroom for the Holy Spirit to convict me of being a weak and wayward Christian.

He caught me by surprise that sweltering summer day as I slumped on the bench about to expire and placed in my imagination the following picture.

> ...I am standing at the steering wheel of a large ship with hundreds of sailors watching me. I am the captain and stare straight ahead into a gray fog. A man surrounded by a bright light offers to steer the ship, but I say, "I am the master of my fate: I am the captain of my soul," a verse I remembered from the poem Invictus...

I liked that poem before I became a Christian. Now I hated it, yet the Holy Spirit showed me that afternoon that I was living it out.

The scene of the ship awakened me to my foolishness. "No, Lord. It's not my way but Your way." I bowed my head and prayed, "You are the captain of my soul. You are the master of my fate. Right here, right now, I rededicate myself to a deeper relationship with You. I will let You live Your life through me no matter how busy I am."

The Holy Spirit did not sing hallelujahs or lift me supernaturally off the bench, but I sensed deep within me that He was back in business in my life. I would no longer be a loner trying to solve the college-merger chaos: He would be my guide. I decided then and there to start listening to Him again and put myself on the back burner.

This was a real vision given to me. But, don't you see, it's your vision also. You're the one who has put God on the back burner. Oh, yes, He's still on the stove, but you've put yourself on the front burner.

You too have ignored the Holy Spirit, and the farther you have distanced yourself from Him, the less you have recognized it. You are the one who needs to ask the Holy Spirit to convict you of drifting so far from God that you can't feel His presence. If you hadn't drifted, you wouldn't be back in jail.

> Stay on the King's Highway. Let the Lord be the captain of your soul and the master of your fate. Let Him live His life through you during the good times and the bad, especially during the bad. Make the right choices. Whenever you are tempted to fall back into the life that landed you in jail, ask the simple question, "What would you have me do here, Lord?"

❖ ◆ ❖

CHAPTER NINE
Give Up Control of Your Life to Jesus

THREE YEARS LATER, MY SECOND VISION ARRIVED. BEFORE I WAS SAVED, I boasted of my self-sufficiency. One of my favorite songs was the classic by Frank Sinatra – *I Did It My Way*. If something good happened to me, it was because I deserved it. If something bad happened, it was someone else's fault. I was indeed the master of my fate and proud of it. What a half-wit I was before the Holy Spirit came into my life with the other half.

One day in a Minneapolis hotel room, sitting on a chair in the middle of the room, I came to grips that Christ really died for me. I admitted that I was sinner, believed He took on my sins and I was forgiven through Him, and chose Him as my Savior and Lord. I walked over from the left side of the cross in Chapter Three to the right side, from lost to saved. So, I surrendered and gave up control of my life. Or did I?

When I accepted Jesus, He asked me to let Him take over. Sometimes the answer was yes; sometimes the old Pat ran the show. Back and forth, He was in control and then I was in control. When He was in control, my life was blessed. When I was in control, I made some bad choices and got myself in troubles of various sorts. I knew it, but there didn't seem to be anything I could do about it. I loved Jesus, but I didn't want to give up complete control of my life. The idea of total submission scared me. One year, when my life was busy, busy, and problems started cropping up like weeds in a garden, I was in full I'll do it my way mode. I desperately needed a lesson from God's classroom. I was driving to Minneapolis when the Holy Spirit showed up with a vision, on a day so unseasonably hot the highway shimmered. This is my journal entry:

> In my imagination, I saw a bright, spacious, airy room on the top floor of a house I was living in. It was not anything I had seen before. In that room were a sprawling mahogany desk, dark oak floors, and Venetian blinds that let the sun filter in. "This must be my spiritual office," I thought, because Jesus was always there. I saw myself entering the room in the morning for an hour of prayer, worship, and Scripture reading. In that way, it mirrored what I actually did. When I left the room, Jesus did not go with me. I heard Him say, "Let Me go with you," but I ignored Him.
>
> One morning, He suggested we tour the rest of the house; I reluctantly agreed. He led me to a small, dark room in a gloomy part of the house. He asked me to open the door, and I saw the inside of the room as He did – dingy and stuffy, with old rusty machinery controlled by shafts, levers, and other regulating mechanisms. I lowered my head in shame when Jesus revealed this was the control room of my self-life, left over from the days before I became a Christian. It was a place familiar to me and comforting, a room in which I spent way too much time.
>
> Jesus looked at me with great sadness; it seemed as if He was about to cry. Without a word, His hand reached out for the key to this room. I hesitated. His hand stayed where it was, with palm upturned. How could I abandon the control room I grew up with? Jesus finally spoke in a gentle voice: "Give Me the key to your life." My hand shook as I handed Him the key. In that instant, I was transported to the edge of a vast ocean, listening to waves lapping on the shore, feeling a soft wind in my face, and sensing absolute freedom.
>
> After what seemed to be an hour, I returned to the control room and stood there with Jesus. He looked deep into my eyes and said with authority, "Let Me destroy this room!" The experience of the ocean had changed my mind about what was best for me. Without hesitation, I answered Him with a nod of my head.

The control room disappeared in a powerful blast, and I found myself back in the spiritual office. It was ten times larger and brighter and fresher than the previous one, and was the only room in the house.

This is another vision that directly applies to you. You want to keep control of your life, yet you are mystified when your way doesn't work out – again. You, as well as me, have to give the key of your control room over to Jesus. I know it's hard. It was for me too. And I find myself too often trying to grab the key back, at the same time praying He won't give it to me again.

If you hold the key to your own life, you are in a room where you make bad choices and end up in jail. If you hand that key over to Jesus, He will bring you into a room that is more grand than anything you have ever experienced. Running your own life hasn't worked out very well for you. Let Him take over, and experience His joy in you.

The Bible has a single plot running through it. Adam and Eve lose the world God had planned for all mankind. Men and women seek to recapture it by hook or by crook, but they fail miserably. God has a plan to restore the world to the glory for which He created it. That plan is in Jesus Christ for all who choose Him as Savior and Lord. "This means the Bible is a book about you and me, whom he also made and lost and continually seeks, so that what holds it together more than anything else is us," as Frederick Buechner says.

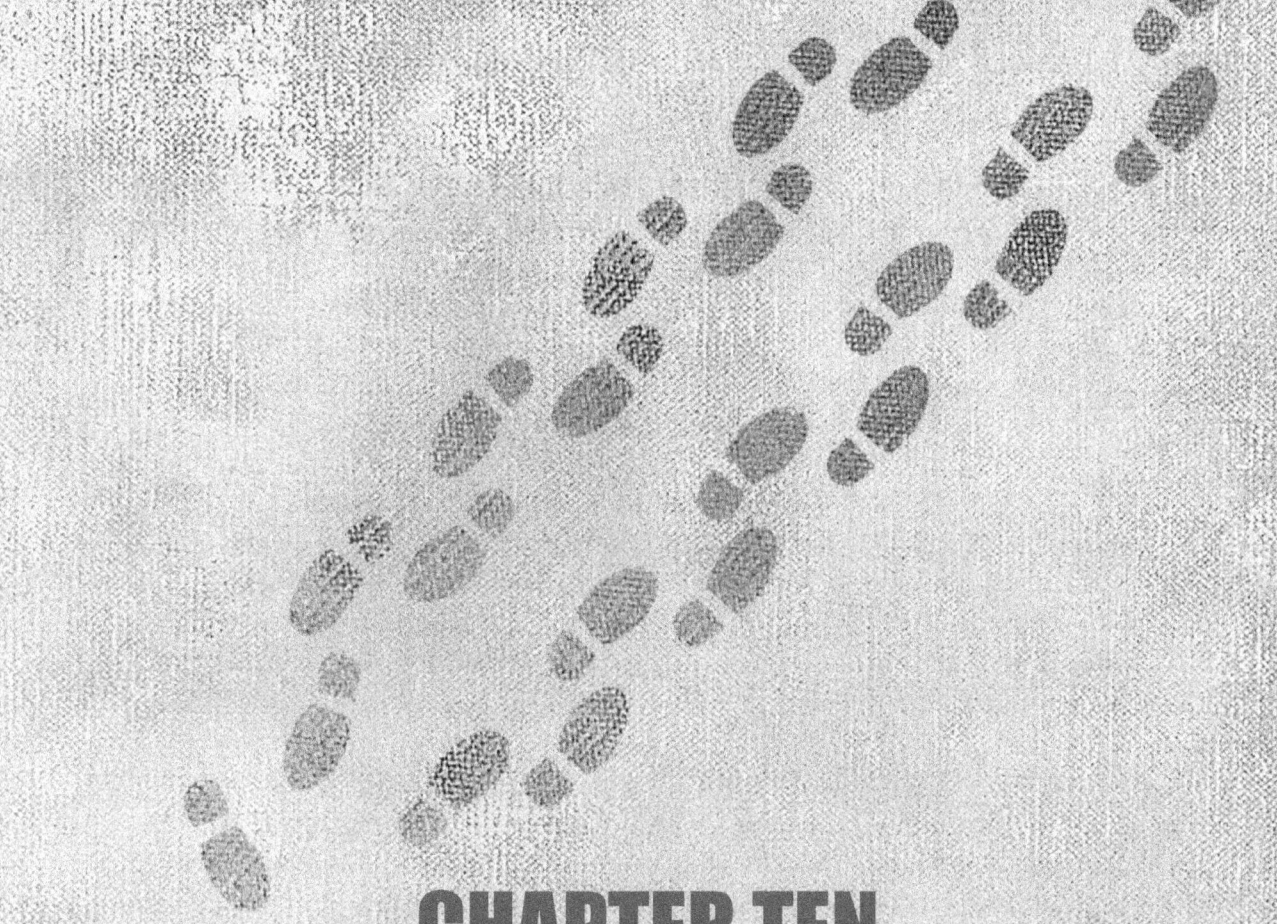

CHAPTER TEN
Turning from Your Way to God's Way

Draw near to God, and He will draw near to you. – James 4:8 (NIV)

WHEN YOU GO YOUR OWN WAY AND THE WAY OF THE WORLD, you are heading in the wrong direction. As long as you stay on your own path, you are on a collision course with the law. Maybe you can make it on your own. Statistics say you can't. You need something more in your life. You need God, and He's waiting for you if you just turn around 180 degrees and head toward Him.

In the military, an officer will command a squad of soldiers to "halt." Then he'll give an order of "about face." Finally, once the squad is turned around, he'll say "forward march." This is the way it is with you. You need to come to a halt in going your own way, then turn around and start marching in God's direction. And as you walk slowly toward Him, He is running toward you.

An interesting concept, but how do you carry it out? Ideas don't do you a lot of good if there isn't some practical way to carry them out. That's the purpose of this final chapter. How do you stay near to God? It's not rocket science or some secret I'm going to give you. You may already know much of this. But you need to move from knowledge to action.

1. READING SCRIPTURE DAILY. Reading the Bible is listening to God. He speaks to you through His Word. But just reading the Bible is not enough. I read through the entire Bible before I became a Christian, but it didn't do me much good. You need to read it through the power and insight of the Holy Spirit, letting the Bible read you, so to speak. Before you start reading, pray something like this, "Holy Spirit, reveal to me today fresh and new ideas and something that can change my life."

2. CONTINUAL PRAYER. "Pray continually" –1 Thessalonians 5:17 (NIV). This means to keep a prayerful attitude all the time. You can praise and worship the Lord and thank Him throughout the day for all He has done for you. You can tell Him how hard it is for you to go His way and ask His Holy Spirit to show you how. Every time you turn to do something new, a very good prayer is to ask, "What would You have me do here, Lord?"

3. PRAYING SCRIPTURE. Did you know you can pray Scripture in addition to reading it? For example, John 15:5 (NIV) says, "Apart from Me you can do nothing." Ask the Holy Spirit to keep you so close to Jesus that everything you do has meaning in His kingdom. Pray that what you do will always be pleasing to Jesus. Don't ask Him to be with you (He always is if you're a believer) but ask Him to show you where He is and then follow Him there.

4. FELLOWSHIP. Surround yourself with Christians who will lift you up instead of tear you down. "As iron sharpens iron, so one person sharpens another" –Proverbs 27.17 (NIV). Be friends with like-minded people. Learn from each other. Have spiritual partners that hold you accountable. Stay away from people and places that are constant temptations. Hang around with men and women who have chosen, like you, to stay out of jail. There is strength in numbers.

5. BIBLE STUDIES. This follows right along with fellowship. You need a firm foundation in Christ to stay out of jail. How can you follow His ways unless you know what they are? How can you love Him unless you know who He is? Chapters 14-17 of the Gospel of John make a wonderful Bible study because they tell you, in Jesus' own words, who He is and why He came. The book of Acts shows the Holy Spirit's intervention in the lives of godly men. The Bible filters out wrong thinking.

6. ATTENDING A SPIRIT-FILLED CHURCH. I've had several people tell me they can be Christians without going to church. That's like saying a person can stay alive on bread and water. Why would you want to do that when good nourishment can be found in churches that are filled with the Holy Spirit's power? I'm not talking about feel-good churches and those who preach a prosperity message, but those who challenge you to live out your Christian faith.

7. SERVICE TO OTHERS IN CHRIST'S NAME. This is one we often miss. "Each of you should use whatever gift you have received to serve others, as faithful stewards of God's grace in its various forms" – 1 Peter 4:10 (NIV). In the parable of the sheep and the goats in Matthew 25 (NIV), Jesus says, "Whatever you did for one of the least of these brothers and sisters of mine, you did for me." I sense a nearness to the Lord when I serve Him by speaking with inmates about how to stay out of jail.

8. LISTENING TO PRAISE AND WORSHIP MUSIC. Praise and worship music is not just something to fill in time before a sermon. It inspires us and uplifts us and puts us in a good frame of mind to hear the message that will be preached later. The music appeals to our emotions and sensations. The sermon is directed to our thinking and the actions we take as a result. We need to be engaged – mind, will, and emotions – to experience all of God.

9. WATCHING AND LISTENING FOR GOD. "The basic reality of God is plain enough. Open your eyes and there it is!" – Romans 1:19. God is behind His creation and if you watch and listen for Him, you will find Him in the people you meet and in the nature you see. You will hear Him in the quietness of your cell and the stillness of your soul. "You will seek me and find me when you seek me with all your heart" – Jeremiah 29:13 (NIV). Will you seek Him with all your heart?

10. LIVING A LIFE OF SURRENDER TO JESUS. Be careful about seeking knowledge for the sake of knowledge. I've run across supposed Christians who talk a good game but don't exhibit the fruits of the Spirit. It's not more knowledge you need. It's more surrender. You can read the Bible until the lights go off and quote Scripture to impress people. But if you're not surrendered to the Lord, you're living in the wrong world – and a return to jail is your destiny.

❖ ◆ ❖

The Final Message

Life has been a tough road for you. Things have not gone your way. You want to change your life around, to go a different way than you have gone in the past. A life free of crime and jail. A life of hope and promise.

> When you're in your own world, you have no resistance to your old way of life. When you're in God's world, He provides the resistance.

You can't make it on your own. You've proven that over and over. You need to throw your old self in the trash bin and stop walking the way that has never worked for you – your own way. You need something new, something revolutionary. You need to follow Jesus Christ every step of the way. You need to walk arm in arm with the Holy Spirit. You need to say, "Here I am. Take me," with all your heart and with all your soul and with all your will.

I hope you don't close this book and say something like, "Those are some good thoughts." Or, "I really liked this book." In a few weeks you'll forget all about it and it won't do you any more good than last week's newspaper.

I pray instead that you will take action based on what is in this book. Start making the right choices. Don't think about walking arm in arm with the Holy Spirit. Do it. Don't think about tearing into the Bible with reckless abandon. Do it. Don't consider praying more often. Do it.

Choose to live at the top of Mobile Bay. Stay in tune with the Holy Spirit Station. Listen for the under melody of the Holy Spirit. Give the keys of your life over to Jesus. Stay on the King's Highway.

Let me make it simpler. Whether you are a Christian or not, you've been going your own way. Stop! Turn around! Start going God's way! It's a choice. It's always been a choice. It doesn't just happen by reading this book or any other book. You've got to muster up all the strength of your heart, mind, will, and emotions and say, "I'll do it!"

❖ ◆ ❖